AURA GARDEN GUIDES

John Mattock

Pruning

AURA BOOKS

Aura Garden Guides

Pruning
John Mattock

© 1997 Advanced Marketing (UK) Ltd.,
Bicester, England

Produced by:
Transedition Limited for
Aura Books, Bicester
and first published in 2002

Editing by:
Asgard Publishing Services, Leeds

Typesetting by:
Organ Graphic, Abingdon

10 9 8 7 6
Printed in Dubai

ISBN 1 901683 19 2

Photographic credits
All photographs by the author
except as follows: J. Glover 4,
28, 33c, 37tr, 41bl; P. McHoy 18,
61, 75; Photos Horticultural title
verso, 9, 12bl/r, 13, 14, 16-17,
17, 20b, 29, 35tl, 38, 41tr, 48, 50,
74, 76br; T. Sandall 6bl, 8tr, 10,
12tl, 20t, 21tl/tr, 22c/b, 23, 24,
25, 26, 26-27, 27, 33tl, 39, 40,
46-47, 52-53, 53, 54, 68, 69,
72b, 72-73; H. Smith 5, 6tr, 7,
8bl, 11, 15, 16, 18-19, 19, 21b,
22tl/tr, 30, 31, 33br, 34, 35br, 36,
37bl, 42, 44, 45, 46, 48-49, 49,
51, 70, 72tl, 76tr/bl

John Mattock, VMH, DHM, is
one of Britain's leading rose
experts. While working for
his family firm he grew half
a million roses annually
and introduced many new
varieties. He served on the
council of the Royal Horticultural Society (RHS) for
many years, and for twelve
years chaired the committee
responsible for the Chelsea
Flower Show. He speaks on
a variety of gardening
subjects and is author of
several horticultural books.
He holds the highest RHS
award, the Victoria Medal
of Honour for services to
horticulture.

CONTENTS

Introduction

From the earliest civilisations, people have attempted to control or manipulate their natural environment. The first plants to be used in this way were herbs, when they were found to be beneficial to people's health and well-being. This led to the creation of the first medicines.

Then, as life became more sophisticated, people began to realise that there were many other plants that could similarly contribute to the quality of their life. At first these were purely functional, providing food and sustenance, or building materials (timber) for the creation of new living spaces. Yet as more and more plants were harnessed to improve the quality of life, so people began to manipulate them simply to create a more pleasurable or interesting environment — hence the evolution of garden plants. At the same time more so-called economic plants were needed to feed and house a rapidly expanding population.

As plant selection, and later plant breeding, became more sophisticated, so new plants could be developed for their decorative or economic value. People soon discovered, however, that these new plants

could not be induced to give their full potential until their growth was in some way physically controlled.

This was particularly so with plants made up of hard, woody material. A fruit tree, for example, could not give of its best unless the growth of the plant was controlled. And this is effectively what pruning is: the manipulation of the fabric of a plant so that it can become more productive.

This book has two main aims:

• to provide a simple guide to obtaining the greatest possible pleasure from pruning;

• coupled with this, to provide a simple understanding of the principles of pruning.

Pruning clematis — it may not look very glamorous at this stage, but the results will justify the effort.

Why prune?

The majority of recently introduced garden plants (i.e. those introduced over the last 200 years) are the culmination, in many instances, of very sophisticated plant breeding and selection. Although originally descended from the wild plants (species) that form part of our natural environment, the modern rose plant, fruit tree or decorative garden shrub has to be cared for and seasonally persuaded (pruned) in order to become the highly productive plant that its breeders intended.

If you have recently taken over a neglected garden, then you will readily understand what is meant by 'overgrown' or mis-shapen plants. And where trees have been hacked at leaving a trail of disaster, you will readily see the need for careful pruning.

The dictionary describes the word 'prune' as follows: 'Trim (tree etc.) by cutting away superfluous branches etc.; lop off, cut away (branches etc.) or figuratively clear what is superfluous. In common with most operations in the garden, pruning is a simple exercise when fully comprehended. Although a certain mystique has almost become the norm in the description of pruning techniques, most of the practice of cutting back and manipulating a plant is common sense. There is very rarely any mystery.

Pruning back spiraea

Fruit trees can be encouraged to be more productive, while rose bushes have the potential to flower for very long periods, and decorative shrubs can be persuaded to conform more effectively to the parameters of the garden.

Plants that should not be pruned

The species or wild forms of most plants require very little attention. On the contrary, pruning can cause real damage to the fabric of a tree or shrub that is growing in the wild.

One only has to think of the barbaric way in which many trees were pollarded years ago to conform to current requirements. In reality it was an admission that a particular species of tree should not have been planted there in the first place.

Such misguided and ignorant procedures are frowned on these days, and in these days of cost-cutting this ugly practice is considered much too labour-intensive. Modern methods call for the elimination of those types of tree or shrub which can only be controlled in this way.

5

Pruning tools

If you are going to prune branches in the correct way, then you must have a selection of tools specifically designed to perform this operation.

Important factors to consider

The most important factor to do with the cutting tools that you buy is the quality of the **cutting edge**, and this is generally reflected in the quality of the steel used. As in most areas of life, you get what you pay for. A cheap instrument can quickly become expensive if it is always in a state of disrepair and demands constant sharpening.

Strict **hygiene** is also essential to prevent the spread of disease.

In some circumstances it can be just as important as the quality of the cutting edge. Before moving from one plant to another, always give a quick wipe-down with surgical spirit — a vital precaution against the possible spread of plant viruses. All tools in the garden shed must of course be thoroughly cleaned, and if necessary lubricated as well.

Knives

With the introduction of modern side-by-side secateurs that produce a quality cut, there is less insistence nowadays on the use of the traditional pruning knife. On the contrary, large pruning knives are very much a thing of the past — which is just as well, as they can be quite lethal and are very dangerous in untrained hands.

Nevertheless, a sharp pocket knife is always useful, and many experienced gardeners would not feel complete if they did not carry this essential tool in their pockets at all times.

Secateurs

Once a very crude instrument, garden secateurs have now become the most sophisticated tool in the gardener's armoury

A pruning saw, a pruning knife, a parrot nose and the ever-present secateurs. Whatever cutting tools you use, always pay strict attention to hygiene. And when buying tools, make sure the cutting blades are of the highest-quality steel.

of equipment. The modern implement is generally known as the side-by-side, and with the benefit of a high-quality cutting edge it can match even the most superior pruning knife.

There are many makes of secateur, but as a general rule, quality is indicated by price. Without a doubt the finest secateurs are those produced by Felco. Such is the sophistication of their product that the makers are able to offer a variety of sizes and adaptations for both left- and right-handed gardeners. They are in continual use by the Royal Horticultural

A pair of modern garden secateurs in use. As with most things in life, you generally find you get what you pay for.

Society (RHS) and the Royal National Rose Society (RNRS), and are available at most gardening shops nationwide and overseas.

There are cheaper copies of the Felco instrument available. There is also a make of secateurs in which the blade cuts onto a flat base. Although effective, this mechanism can produce a bruise on the side of the stem that comes in contact with the non-cutting edge, and this in turn tends to encourage die-back.

Saws

There is a vast selection of pruning saws available, ranging from a small pocket-size model with a folding blade to large bow saws for the heavier branches.

Their merit is qualified by the work they are required to do. The smaller versions are particularly adapted for removing old wood in shrubs and roses, where accessibility is at a premium.

Long arms

Sometimes called a **parrot nose**, these are secateurs that have been specially developed for removing small branches that would otherwise be out of reach for ordinary pruning purposes.

This tool can also be used for cutting the odd bloom or fruit normally out of reach by other means. Long arms are light to use and are available in a variety of handle lengths.

Tree pruners

These are a heavier form of long arms. With the help of extensions they are capable of reaching as far as 12 ft (4 m). However, in order to use them you must have strong arms and ample space to accommodate falling branches safely.

For the more sophisticated gardener there is a mechanically driven form of this instrument. But beware — in the hands of the untrained user this tool can be positively dangerous.

Tree pruners can be extremely useful, but require a lot of strength to manoeuvre and may be dangerous in inexperienced hands.

Gloves

A pair of good-quality leather gloves is of paramount importance for pruning. Plastic gloves are a waste of time as they lack ventilation and have very little resistance to thorns.

Good leather gloves that are supple but tough are hard to

7

A really stout pair of gloves is essential for pruning. The non-active hand especially needs protection from thorns and other hazards.

find but will prove well worth the trouble and search. If poor-quality leather becomes wet through, it dries out to become hard and therefore uncomfortable to wear.

You should also avoid gloves with a soft inside lining, as this is difficult to dry out and guaranteed to absorb some of the more uninviting odours of the human body.

Gardening can sometimes be a dangerous pastime and infection (blood poisoning) must always be avoided. Most professionals will not hold tools with a gloved hand, yet always take care to handle material with the non-active hand or limb protected by a strong pair of gloves.

Wound paints

There was a practice at one time of treating plant wounds with some form of protective paint;

grafting wax was also recommended. Recent research has proved conclusively that these nostrums are of little avail and indeed can encourage disease. A non-toxic wood preservative might just solve this problem but Mother Nature appears to be quite competent at healing its own wounds.

Hedge trimmers

A recent innovation is the practice of cutting back roses with hand or mechanical hedge trimmers. While there is now some doubt about the efficacy of this technique, mechanical hedge trimmers are nonetheless very useful in trimming hedges and can save a tremendous amount of time.

However, like all pruning equipment they must be well maintained and the blades kept sharp. In the hands of the untrained they can also be extremely dangerous.

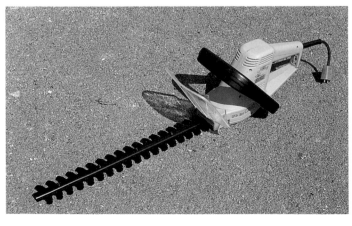

Hedge trimmers can be very useful for trimming hedges, but there is some doubt as to their efficacy in any of the more usual pruning procedures. And they must be handled with great care to avoid the risk of serious injury.

Types of pruning

For the purposes of describing the various methods of pruning, it is prudent to divide these methods into different forms or categories. Each type of pruning can make a positive contribution to the productiveness of plants, whether in flower, in fruit or both.

Formative pruning
Literally speaking, one could call formative pruning the construction of a plant to create the most pleasing shape and yield the most effective display of fruits and flowers. The main thrust of domestic gardening is to control the fabric of a plant and at the same time prevent the whole exercise from becoming a chore.

There are all sorts of ways you can prune a plant to its best advantage. It may mean eliminating the main shoot or leader to produce a more bushy plant. More often than not, particularly with wall plants, it may mean not only cutting out various branches but also training the remaining branches to grow in specific directions, so that new growth is properly dispersed and covers the wall area as effectively as possible.

Hard and light pruning
These terms are used to indicate the severity with which a stem or a whole plant is cut back.

Many trees that produce soft fruits have to be severely cut back to encourage new and productive growth. With some rambling roses, the old flowering wood has to be eliminated or at least reduced to encourage new flowering wood of the best quality and potential.

Light pruning is more commonly associated with training a plant, usually immediately after flowering. In many cases this means no more than the dead-heading of spent flowers, which is a common practice during the milder periods of the year when the plant is in full growth.

Seasonal pruning
Many plants have to be pruned at specific times of year. For example, where non-productive growth (usually old flowering wood) has to be removed to make way for new growth, this generally has to be done during periods of dormancy or in early spring. Such a procedure usually applies to plants such roses, vines, some climbing plants and occasionally ornamental shrubs.

This dogwood, which has been badly neglected, is being cut back quite severely so as to encourage new, more productive growth.

What is a good cut?

Pruning by definition involves the removal of twigs and branches, which in turn implies that a sharp instrument must be used to effect the operation. But there is considerable debate as to how the quality of the cut affects the subsequent wound or scar — and hence the effectiveness of the pruning operation in the long term.

Horticultural experts are now generally agreed that the old practice of dressing scars with various nostrums such as grafting wax and wound paint have proved to be ineffective. On the contrary, in certain circumstances they may even prove positively detrimental to rapid recovery and the encouragement of further growth.

A slice, not a chop

There is one aspect of pruning that remains undisputed: the orientation of the cut is paramount, irrespective of whether you use a pair of secateurs, a pruning knife or a saw.

The reasons for this can be found in the structure of wood itself. The texture of timber is best described by carpenters when they speak of cutting either 'across the grain' or 'with the grain'.

For a gardener this means that a branch or stem should be cut

obliquely rather than straight across. In other words it should be sliced rather than chopped.

Perhaps the best example one could follow when practising this vital technique is that of a skilled hedger at work in the country. It can be such a delight to watch him as he slices branches with such ease.)

Practical evidence suggests that the wounds created by an oblique cut tend to heal much more quickly. One contributory factor is that water is less likely to accumulate here than on a flat-chopped surface, and this helps to discourage the development of fungal spores.

To sum up, then, a sliced cut is not only easier to achieve than a straight chop, but is also much better for the general health of the plant.

The 'perfect' cut

There is less insistence on perfection these days than used to be the case. If wood is removed immediately above an eye or a leaf, then so much the better, but this factor is no longer considered to be so vitally important. Besides, where stems are small there are very few gardeners with sufficiently acute eyesight to achieve the 'perfect' cut.

Left *Skilful pruning is necessary to produce such a glorious display of apple blossom.*

Right *Pruning a rose branch with a pair of secateurs — a slice is always better than a straight chop.*

An oblique or sliced cut

When you cut back a branch, or indeed any woody stem, it is much easier to slice it at an angle than to cut it straight across. This is because an oblique cut corresponds more closely to the structure of the plant cells in the woody structure of the branch.

A cut made at an angle will also heal more quickly. Moreover, moisture is less likely to accumulate on a slanting surface, which means that fungus spores are less likely to multiply.

The closer you make the cut to an eye or a bud, the better the result — though gardeners are less fanatical about this than they once were.

Remember that successful clean cuts like these can only be obtained by using very sharp tools.

A saw cut

When cutting bigger branches, you will probably find that a straight saw cut is the only practical solution. But it must be neatly finished by trimming it clean so as to speed up the healing process.

Left *This spur-pruned apple branch has been cut immediately above a leaf node — though nowadays the exact site of a cut is considered less vital than it used to be.*

Right *After a saw cut you should trim the wound clean to help the healing process. Make sure you use a sharp knife for this purpose.*

Bigger branches

Removing major branches with a saw can be a trifle hazardous if you have insufficient experience of handling such a tool.

Nevertheless, the rudiments of using a saw are easy to understand. You should always make an initial cut underneath the branch closer to the main stem than the principle point of severance. This simple exercise will be sufficient to prevent the skinning or tearing of the trunk as the branch falls. You should also ensure that no damage or

Pruning a cotoneaster with the aid of a small pruning saw

Severing major branches without damaging the tree

Care is essential when severing major branches with a saw. If the task is sloppily executed, this will not only be dangerous to life and limb, but can also be very disfiguring to the tree.

There is a wrong way (top) and a right way (bottom) of cutting off a branch. Saw off the branch flush with the trunk, and start by making an initial cut underneath at the point where you intend to cut from above. This will prevent the bark skinning when the branch is nearly severed (which creates ugly scars), and there will be no die-back (which encourages infection).

For the sake of safety, you must also ensure that the severed branch will fall freely without damaging other plants (or human beings).

If a branch is very big, it should be removed with a mechanical chain saw — a job that should be handed over to a professional tree surgeon.

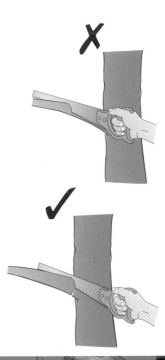

injury will occur as it tumbles to the ground.

If you need to remove bigger branches a long way above ground level, then a safety harness is essential, particularly if you plan on using a mechanical saw for the purpose.

The paramount criterion in any operation requiring the severance of plant material must be the quality of the tools used. A very sharp and efficient cutting edge is not only essential but it makes for easier handling and greater job satisfaction.

Another way to stop the branch from splitting or tearing as it is finally severed is to support it from below — provided of course that it is not too heavy for this.

Shapes and sizes

The majority of our fruit and ornamental trees will grow and develop into conventional shapes and sizes with very little persuasion, but they will not necessarily give satisfaction. Fruit trees, for example, may be lacking in productivity, while in many instances ornamentals will not grow to the most helpful size, especially in a small garden, where space is at a premium.

All of the shapes introduced are illustrated by photos so that you can become familiar, not only with the shapes and sizes which can be achieved, but also with the names that are used to describe them.

Ornamentals

The majority of ornamental trees and shrubs will grow into natural forms and demand the minimum of discipline. But is nonetheless important to be familiar with the descriptions that are used.

Spreading forms

Many of the ornamental cherries, after their spring display of colour, will develop into broad canopies of shade in the summer. They are therefore typical of this shape of tree. Although attractive, they can often occupy a lot of space.

Ornamental trees with a spreading habit

This shape is commonly associated with ornamental cherries and chestnut trees, and is generally accepted as contributing to the plant architecture and beauty of gardens.

It is not, however, advisable in a small garden, where a spreading tree can exclude valuable light.

The large size and spreading habit of Acer *pseudoplatanus 'Brilliantissimum'* **(left)** *makes it unsuitable for growing in a small garden.* Hebe *'Midsummer Beauty'* **(right)** *is less typical of this form, but is easier to accommodate and equally beautiful in its own way.*

Pyramidal forms

This shape is associated with formal plantings in urban developments, where uniform shape is the ultimate criterion. Many conifers are naturally pyramidal in shape, and a tendency to produce rogue, uneven and unsightly branches is not the norm.

Ornamental trees with a pyramidal habit

This is probably the most photogenic of tree shapes. Many conifers, including Norway spruce (*Picea abies*) used for Christmas trees, will mature naturally to this shape and require very little maintenance.

A glorious pyramidal specimen — Ilex × altaclarensis *'Camellifolia Variegata'*

15

Cotoneaster *'Hybridus Pendulus'* — the Latin word *'pendulus'* is normally indicative of a weeping habit.

Conical forms

There are many trees that assume a conical shape as they grow into maturity, but the classic conical form is generally associated with solitary specimen conifers gracing broad landscapes. Like pyramidal forms, trees with a conical habit have the advantage of being relatively easy to maintain.

Ornamental trees with a weeping habit

The majority of weeping trees require very little maintenance. On the contrary, trimming branches may be detrimental to their development into plants of great beauty.

Their pendulous growth structure makes weeping trees prone to shedding small broken branches. But this is no more than a nuisance, and as such only requires regular tidying up.

Weeping forms

Botanists will point out that weeping forms are common among a wide range of trees, but by far the most familiar one to be found in British gardens is the weeping willow (*Salix babylonica*).

Weeping forms are available for a variety of trees, providing an excellent opportunity to introduce new shapes to a garden. Their weeping habit develops naturally, although meticulous staking is essential in young plants.

Picea glauca *var.* albertiana *'Conica'* — conical and pyramidal shapes are perhaps commonest among the coniferous trees.

Ornamental trees with a conical habit

This beautiful natural form is common in many gardens, and is probably the most maintenance-free of all the tree shapes.

Conical trees can vary in size from dwarf forms to the tallest of conifers.

Round-headed forms

Though generally associated with apple trees in the small garden, this shape is more commonly observed with specimen oaks.

This English walnut (Juglans regia) is an example of a round-headed tree in the wild — though our native oaks (Quercus robur) are among the best representatives of this shape.

Ornamental trees with a round-headed habit

In its natural form, this is the most stately-looking of all large trees. Oaks, which naturally evolve into this shape, are a magnificent sight. Large limbs are occasionally prone to die-back, but these must be skilfully removed by a tree surgeon — not a job for the amateur.

Cedrus deodara *'Golden Horizon'* is
a conifer with an arching habit.

Ornamental trees with an arching habit

Palm trees are the typical plant of this shape. Contrary to informed opinion, they do require occasional maintenance. At least once every two years the older lower branches must be removed as they age. Otherwise they will become unsightly and liable to fall, creating a hazard in the garden.

Arching forms

This is not a shape generally associated with trees in this country, though it is possible to train some roses to develop an arching branching structure (see page 62). The arching fronds of a palm tree are more familiar in warmer climates such as that of the Mediterranean region.

Columnar forms

This is very good shape for using in small gardens where space is at a premium. There are columnar varieties of many different trees, ranging from ornamental maples and cherries (see picture) to the new Ballerina apple trees.

Ornamental trees with a columnar habit

Although this shape is usually associated with the Lombardy poplar (*Populus nigra* 'Italica'), it is now more easily recognised with some forms of decorative cherry (see picture) or small-growing apples such as the Ballerina. This shape requires little maintenance other than cutting back vigorous laterals.

Prunus *'Amanogawa'* is a beautiful
ornamental cherry noted for its
columnar habit.

Fruit trees

Fruit trees are by definition cultivated to produce the best crop of fruit commensurate with their shape and size, particularly where they are grown in restricted areas.

There is a very wide range of fruit tree shapes, all of them the product of very careful formative pruning. The overriding factor, particularly with apples and plums, is the grafting stock upon which the trees have been propagated, and which can dramatically effect the potential of the plant and its fruiting capability.

The actual pruning methods used are described in detail later under the headings of apples, pears, peaches etc.

Standard

The standard tree has for a long time been the conventional form used for the majority of fruit trees. But it requires strong staking when the tree is first planted, followed by judicious pruning to develop a large enough plant. It is considered

A standard whitebeam (Sorbus aria) — despite being the traditional form used for most fruit trees, the standard is uneconomical in commercial terms and too large to be accommodated in small gardens.

somewhat passé in commercial establishments because pruning and harvesting are so labour-intensive. A standard tree is certainly inappropriate in small gardens. The trunk grows to about 7 ft (over 2 m).

19

Half-standard

This form is identical in shape to the full standard, but easier to cultivate and harvest because the branches and fruit are much more accessible. The trunk usually measures about 4 ft (over 1 m) in height.

A handsome example of a half-standard apple tree — so much easier to cultivate and harvest than the more traditional standard form.

Now almost bare of foliage, this apple bush provides an excellent opportunity to examine the characteristic branching structure.

Bush

This is the most popular form of fruit tree, both in small gardens and in 'pick your own' establishments. If it is propagated on a dwarfing rootstock, then formative pruning is all that is needed to produce a tree that is

not only easy to control but has a great potential for bearing high-quality fruit.

Spindlebush
A spindlebush is in effect a small tree, but the branches are restricted so as to radiate from a central leader growing to about 7 ft (over 2 m) from ground level; the lower trunk measures about 18 in (50 cm).

Cordon
This form is developed as a single stem, and is generally grown at a 45-degree angle. Cordons, which are productive of very high-quality fruit, are normally planted against a wall or fence.

Above *Here are two pictures of the same spindlebush apple — first with its spring blossom (**left**) and later with its autumn fruit (**right**).*

Below *Apple cordons are typically grown in long, serried ranks, but these are less typical in that they have not been grown against a wall or fence.*

Above *A double cordon formed within a double cordon*

Right *A fan-trained fruit tree growing against a fence*

Double cordon
This shape is normally grown in an upright mode, and requires considerable skill and patience to produce.

Fan
The fan is associated with the cultivation of peaches and nectarines. The branches of the fan are trained from the main stem, usually across the surface of a wall or fence. Fans are normally extended to a width of about 10-15 ft (3-5 m).

Espalier
This form is made up of matching pairs of horizontal branches, carefully trained from a central main stem to create a very formal pattern. Espaliers are usually associated with apples and pears.

Centre *A young espalier in blossom*

Bottom *A more mature espalier*

Fruit trees and bushes

Fruit trees, by the systematic control of their growth, can be encouraged to produce an abundance of fruit that is also of the highest quality.

However, the ultimate result will depend on the stock on which cultivars (cultivated varieties) have been propagated. This may range in size from very dwarfing, through bush, to small trees and larger trees.

The eventual size of the tree can also be determined by formative pruning, and its shape by training into, for example, a cordon, an espalier or a fan.

The other factor that will influence the method of pruning is the way that the fruit is borne. Some varieties will bear fruit on the shoot tips, whereas others are more prolific if they are encouraged to be spur-bearers.

Apples
Malus sylvestris cultivars

Formative pruning is of the essence, not only for small gardens fortunate enough to accommodate bush fruit, but also for those blessed with walls and fences that are ideal for cordons, espaliers and fans.

Once the outline has been established, a strict attention to seasonal pruning will yield an abundant crop that is of superior quality.

Bush forms

Once you have established a good plant, you should concentrate on developing healthy two-year-old fruit-bearing wood. With spur-bearing trees this can normally be achieved by cutting back in the summer to establish hard flowering wood for the following season's crop (see also panel overleaf). Any winter pruning should be limited to formative pruning — thinning out any overcrowded growth and maintaining an open structure to the bush.

Half-standards and standards

The principle objective with these forms to achieve a well-spaced open-structured tree. This can be achieved quite simply by removing small lateral stems and scrubby wood. Neglected trees must be heavily thinned to prevent overcrowding and to assist in the control of disease problems.

A columnar apple tree

23

Cordons, espaliers and fans

These forms of tree should normally have been trained before they are delivered to you from a nursery or garden centre. While it is vital to maintain the overall structure, summer pruning of lateral growth is essential to promote fruit-bearing wood. Spur-bearing varieties are suitable for these methods of culture. Tip-bearers are difficult to train.

Ashmead's Kernel

Lord Lambourne

Spur-pruning apples

When pruning fruit trees, the primary object is to stimulate new fruiting branches (stems). In most apple varieties that are grown as standards or bushes, this is achieved by spur pruning — i.e. cutting back vigorous lateral growths but at the same time thinning out over-crowded stems and branches that are crossing. Older shoots that have already borne fruit should also be controlled.

Training a cordon apple

This structure is in reality a maiden plant trained at an oblique angle. The process may already have begun before the plant left the nursery. The principle object of pruning (once the structure of the plant is established) is to control lateral growth. In the formative years, the main task (right) is winter pruning of lateral growths.

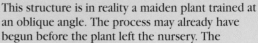

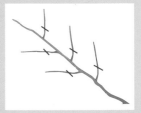

Controlling extraneous growths from laterals (left) is a summer exercise.

Some tip-bearing apples

	Dessert	Culinary
Early	Discovery Irish Peach Tyderman's Early Worcester	none
Mid-season	Lord Lambourne St Edmund's Pippin Worcester Pearmain	Golden Noble
Late	Cornish Gillyflower	Bramley's Seedling

Training a double cordon

Initially trained from a maiden plant, the whip is reduced to about 1 ft (30 cm) from the ground. When two of the strongest laterals have grown and developed hard wood, tie them at an angle of about 45 degrees, and subsequently at about 30 degrees. Once they have reached a length of about 18-24 in (45-60 cm), start to train them vertically. After that, treat any subsequent growth as you would for a single cordon.

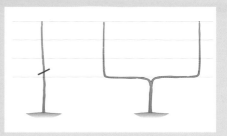

Training an espalier

First cut back a young whip as for a cordon. Then, as new growth develops, train two laterals and allow a central leader to grow. Repeat the same procedure the following season, and the season after that, and so on. Although there is no limit to the size of the plant, three or four tiers is often the most practical arrangement.

first year *second year* *fourth year*

Some spur-bearing apples

	Dessert	**Culinary**
Early	Beauty of Bath	George Neal
	Epicure	Lord Suffield
	George Cave	
Mid-season	Cox's Orange Pippin	Blenheim Orange
	Egremont Russet	Golden Noble
	Fortune	Norfolk Beauty
	Ribstone Pippin	Rev. W. Wilks
	Sunset	
Late	Ashmead's Kernel	Bountiful
	Claygate Pearmain	Wellington
	D'Arcy Spice	Encore
	Kidd's Orange Red	Monarch
	Orleans Reinette	Newton Wonder
	Tyderman's Late Orange	

Orleans Reinette

25

Pears
Pyrus communis cultivars

The pruning of pears is essentially much the same as that of apples (see preceding pages). Pears, however, are more productive in warmer conditions. Both apples and pears benefit from a short, sharp winter, which makes them highly productive.

The majority of pears are spur-bearing and will therefore appreciate young growth being systematically cut back by two-thirds every year. Also, the regular thinning of old stubs and branches will encourage high-quality fruit.

Pear fruits by their very nature need to be harvested as they mature, and will ripen quickly after picking.

This large pear espalier trained against a fence will become highly productive in the summer.

An espalier pear in blossom — pear trees require essentially the same treatment as apples.

Some recommended pears (all spur-bearing)

	Dessert	Culinary
Early	Beth Clapp's Favourite Doyenne d'Eté Williams Bon Chrétien	none
Mid-season	Beurré Hardy Beurré Superfin Conference Doyenne du Comice Fondance d'Automne Marie Louise Pitmaston Duchess	Beurré Clairgeau
Late	Beurré d'Anjou Glou Morceau Olivier de Serres Winter Nells	Black Worcester Catillac Vicar of Winkfield

Plums, gages, damsons and bullaces
Prunus cultivars

A Victoria plum fan trained against a garden fence — as with all plums and their relatives, the fan must never be pruned in winter.

The stone fruits that come within this category vary greatly in both appearance and origin, but they all require similar pruning and cultivation techniques.

Most can be grown as a bush or half-standard, or trained to form a pyramid or fan. The shape, growth and adaptability of a plant depends to a certain extent on the rootstock. Fruit is normally produced at the base of one-year-old growth and on two-year-old wood and spurs.

The most important thing is to observe the no-cutting rule during the winter months, thereby reducing or eliminating the risk of a fungal disease known as silver leaf.

Bush
Young cultivars should be encouraged to develop a strong fabric and grow into well-proportioned plants. You should allow three or four well-spaced leading shoots to develop, and then prune them back to about two-thirds.

Eventually lateral shoots will develop to form the basic framework. This fabric can then be controlled by shortening strong leaders. After that you should carry out an annual removal of all weak, damaged or badly placed laterals.

Established plum fans
Over-exuberant lateral growths should be controlled by cutting them back by one-half. You can maintain a good distribution of young growth by tying in an advantageous stem if required.

Half-standards and standards
Encourage strong leaders which can then be cut back by one-half to produce strong laterals. Once the fabric of the tree is established, strong growth must be reduced by one-half. After that, some branches have to be removed completely to avoid overcrowding.

Damsons and bullaces
These two cousins of the plum have a relatively simple ancestry, and are really varieties of

the wild species. They enjoy a long lifespan and appear to thrive in more rugged situations. Nevertheless, basic maintenance — such as the removal of broken branches and reduction of poor lateral growth — will improve productivity.

As with all plums and their various cousins, the cardinal rule is never to prune or cut branches during the winter season, and also to reduce aged scrubby growth so as to maintain a healthy plant.

Recommended damsons

Early	Merryweather
Mid-season	Bradley's King Farleigh
Late	Frogmore Damson Shropshire

This Farleigh damson has provided an abundant crop of fruit. In general, damsons and bullaces will thrive even in the poorest conditions, but like all fruit trees they are more productive if basic pruning measures are carried out.

Some recommended plums and gages

	Dessert	Culinary
Early	Early Laxton Opal Stint	Czar Early Rivers Pershore
Mid-season	Allgrove's Superb Black Gold Cambridge Gage Early Transparent Gage Jefferson Kirkes Old Greengage Victoria	Belle de Louvain Cox's Emperor Purple Pershore
Late	Coe's Golden Drop Laxton's Delight Purple Gage Santa Rosa Washington	Giant Prune Marjorie's Seedling Warwickshire Drooper

Recommended apricots

Early	Early Moorpark Hemskerk New Large Early
Mid-season	Alfred Breda Farmingdale
Late	Moorpark Shipley's

Apricots
Prunus armeniaca cultivars

These fruit trees are notoriously difficult to grow in this country. They enjoy a brief cold winter followed by a spring that is free of early frosts. Apricots flower very early, and are generally happier on warm walls, trained as fans.

The golden rule, as with the majority of stone fruits (plums etc.), is never to prune during the winter months, when open wounds invite infection from silver leaf. Young, vigorous shoots can be trained across walls to extend the fabric of the plant. But in all other situations this growth should be cut back to encourage sound blossom-bearing wood.

A sunny limestone wall in the Northamptonshire village of Aynho provides the ideal situation for this Moorpark apricot. However, apricots are notoriously difficult to grow in Great Britain, where winters are sometimes long and spring weather is often so capricious.

Cherries
Prunus avium and
P. cerasus cultivars

These are conveniently divided into sweet cherries (*P. avium* cultivars) and acid or culinary forms (*P. cerasus* cultivars). The cherries are not very demanding of too much attention. The voracious appetite of birds is generally the greatest problem.

Sweet cherries
Fan-trained sweet cherries will yield the finest-quality fruit, but

29

Pruning a Morello cherry

The principle aim when pruning a Morello cherry is to encourage the production of one-year-old wood. (In this respect it differs from sweet cherries, which fruit on two-year-old laterals.)

The best way to achieve this is by heavy feeding (nitrogen and potash) and the systematic removal of ageing lateral shoots. All cutting must be done in late spring and early summer to reduce the incidence of leaf curl.

Cut back fruiting laterals almost to the main stem to encourage new growth.

they also need lots of protection from marauding blackbirds.

Young growth can be trained to encourage a good well-balanced plant. These cherries will benefit from an occasional thinning to remove old wood. This must be done in late spring and summer to prevent the depredations of silver leaf.

Acid (culinary) cherries

Acid cherries differ considerably from their sweet cousins in that they bear fruit on one-year-old wood produced the previous year. For this reason they should be pruned in the spring and summer, when older limbs should be removed so as to encourage a greater continuity of new wood.

Some recommended cherries

	Sweet	Culinary (acid)
Early	Early Rivers Waterloo	none
Mid-season	Merton Bigarreau Merton Glory Sunburst	none
Late	Lapins Merton Favourite Noir de Guben Stella	Montmarency Morello Nabella

*A Morello cherry in blossom —
culinary cherry trees are generally
smaller than the sweet cherries,
making them more suitable for
growing in a garden.*

Quinces
Cydonia oblonga cultivars

Quinces are generally grown as bushes and occasionally as fans. The hard fruits are often apple-shaped but more commonly pear-shaped. They have a heavy aromatic perfume, and are used for making jellies and flavouring fruit dishes.

Once you have achieved a well-established open framework, quinces require little regular pruning other than occasional thinning to maintain the open structure.

Popular cultivars are 'Meeche's Prolifi' and 'Vranja'. It is possible to grow these from cuttings taken in the autumn.

A quince bush in fruit

Recommended varieties of peach and nectarine

Early	Amsden June
	Duke of York
	Earliglo
	Early Alexander
	J. H. Hale
	Saturne
	Waterloo
Mid-season	Bonanza
	Crimson Galande
	Peregrine
	Red Haven
	Rochester
	Royal George
Late	Barrington
	Bellegarde
	Dymond

Peaches and nectarines
Prunus persica cultivars

Peaches and nectarines (the smooth-skinned form of the peach) will grow in temperate climates but must have a warm position free of early spring frosts (see also greenhouse-grown peaches on page 45).

A free-standing bush can occasionally produce a crop, but an espalier or fan with the benefit of a warm wall will give greater satisfaction, particularly if the early flower is protected with a framework of wood supporting a polythene shelter.

This can be used to protect the plant from late autumn through to late spring; it encourages fruit set and inhibits the development of peach leaf curl.

Bush forms
These should develop to produce an open-branched framework. Lateral growths should be shortened in the summer. Peaches produce fruit on two-year-old wood.

Fan-trained peaches
Young plants are generally available from nurseries and garden centres with the rudi-

31

ments of a fan shape already formed. You should encourage further growth by tying in young shoots and cutting back lateral growths in the summer to about one leaf. Occasionally old shoots have to be removed to maintain a good rotation of young wood.

Developing a fan-trained peach

The majority of young trained plants are established before they leave the nursery, but this is not always the case.

The method of training is quite simple. When a young plant is making good stems, remove the central leader. This is essential, otherwise the plant will become too big and unmanageable. Allow the laterals to develop, and tie them back. After about three years the lower limbs have the potential to bear fruit. You can encourage this by cutting back young shoots in early summer and pinching out secondary growth.

first year

second year

third year

established plant

Above *A peach fan trained against a fence*

Right *The fruits of the medlar tree look very decorative against the reddening autumn foliage.*

Medlars
Mespilus germanica

The medlar tree is sometimes described as a relic of a more generous age, as it was more popular in late Victorian times. The fruits, which are harvested in late autumn, are nowadays used in preserves and wine-making; the flavour is considered an acquired taste.

Once they have been picked, the fruits have to be given time for maturing (bletting); they resemble small apples, usually measuring about 2 in (4.5 cm) across with prominent calyces.

Medlars are normally available as half-standards or standards. They should be developed in a similar fashion to apples, allowing open growth and removing overcrowded and diseased branches.

Figs
Ficus carica cultivars

A fig tree enjoys a sunny position in the garden. It is most productive either when trained as a fan or when grown in pot, where its roots can be restricted and it can be moved inside during cold weather.

In a cool climate such as that of the UK, a fig tree will not require much pruning once the plant has become established. Remove all crowded and crossing branches, and any stems damaged by frost.

Recommended figs

Early	Black Ischia
	St John's
	White Marseilles
Mid-season	Brown Turkey
	Brunswick
	Negro Largo

A fig tree grown against a wall

A standard mulberry

Cobnuts and filberts
Corylus avellana and *C. maxima*

These bushes are easy to grow. They tolerate hard conditions and give great satisfaction with their clusters of catkins — usually the first harbingers of spring. The filbert has a husk that envelopes the nut, while the cobnut (hazelnut) has a husk which normally does not.

Cobnuts and filberts are grown as open-centred bushes with eight to twelve branches. You should keep the base of the plants free of side-shoots, and encourage a framework of top-growth by cutting or pinching the strongest branches.

In order to encourage heavier crops, a technique known as 'brutting' is used. In late

The fruit of the filbert

summer the longer side-shoots are broken (but not severed) at about 12 in (30 cm), which appears to encourage a greater profusion of female flowers. When the catkins appear, the broken branches are further shortened to three or four buds. Old and overcrowded branches are also removed.

Mulberries
Morus nigra

These trees are grown commercially for their foliage, which is harvested for silkworms. The fruit has a pleasant enough flavour, but the stains from over-ripe fruit can be ruinous to clothing.

If grown as a half-standard, the mulberry is propagated on its own roots. Once a good framework has developed it will require no seasonal pruning. If branches have to be removed, this must be done when the tree is fully dormant, as the wood bleeds profusely at other times. If bleeding should occur, cauterisation is the only solution.

'Brutting' a cobnut

As an indigenous species cobnuts (hazels) are considered to require little or no seasonal care. They can, however, be encouraged to increase their productivity by the simple process of 'brutting' in the late summer.

This means is breaking (but not severing) strong side-shoots of the current season's growth at about half their length. This appears to increase the production of female flowers.

In winter these stems should be shortened, and extraneous

growth thinned out, to reduce overcrowding.

Recommended walnuts

Broadview
Buccaneer
Franquette
Lara
Marbot
Parisienne

Almonds
Prunus dulcis cultivars

Although almonds are popular in this country as ornamentals, they require frost-free winters in order to produce the fruits from which the nuts are obtained. An established bush produces nuts on one-year-old wood. A quarter of the old shoots should be removed in the summer to encourage fresh growth.

Walnuts
Juglans regia cultivars

This popular nut tree is widely grown in the UK. It thrives on a slightly chalky soil and is grown in gardens as a standard.

Young walnut plants must be encouraged to develop a well-balanced framework. Over-crowded or crossing branches can be eliminated during the winter months.

Once a tree has become established, little pruning is required. On the other hand, it may be many years before the tree starts bearing fruit.

A solitary walnut in the country — in gardens it is normally grown as a standard.

The green fruits of the almond require frost-free winters. The plant is therefore more popular as an ornamental in Great Britain.

Recommended almonds

Ayles
Ferrandel
Ferragnes
Guara
Steliette

Soft fruits

Blackberries and hybrid berries
Rubus fruticosus cultivars and *Rubus* hybrids

The lax growth of these plants means they need to be supported on a wall or fence, with horizontal wires spaced about 12 in (30 cm) apart.

The fruits are produced on one-year-old canes, so you have to remove the old canes which have been harvested in the autumn. Pruning therefore entails cutting out the old canes at the base and tying in the new growths. There is usually an abundance new shoots, so only the strongest should be tied in.

When spring comes, you should cut back any frost-damaged shoots.

Pruning blackberries

Established plants are very productive on one-year-old wood. With such a vigorous plant it is a good idea to encourage continuity of growth. This can best be achieved by retaining new canes as they are produced, temporarily tying them in (see illustration).

Then, immediately after the fruit has been harvested, the old canes should be cut off at ground level, and the new wood realigned and tied in (see illustration).

Some recommended blackberries

Early Bedford Giant
Himalaya Giant
Merton Early
Merton Thornless

Late Ashton Cross
John Innes
Oregon Thornless
Smooth Stem
Thornfree

These blackberries are growing all over the place, and would benefit from some support.

Some recommended hybrid berries

Early	Boysenberry
	Loganberry
	Tayberry
	Veitchberry
Late	none

Highbush blueberries
Vaccinium corymbosum cultivars

This plant is more commonly associated with the United States, but it can be grown in this country with considerable success. Provided the soil is sufficiently acid (i.e. with a pH of 4-5.5), the plants will develop into bushes of between 4 ft and 6 ft (1.5-2 m) in height.

Flowering occurs on two- to three-year-old wood. Pruning

Above *An excellent harvest of blueberries*

Left *A loganberry trained on a pergola can be decorative as well as providing tasty fruit.*

should therefore be restricted to cutting out thin, spindly wood and systematically removing ageing wood to encourage the regular production of new wood grown from the base of the plant.

Recommended highbush blueberries

Early	Bluecrop
	Bluetea
	Patriot
Mid-season	Berkeley
	Herbert
	Ivanhoe
Late	Coville
	Darrow
	Jersey

Blackcurrants
Ribes nigrum cultivars

Blackcurrants are a popular garden crop, thriving in cool conditions on a good fertile soil. They produce the maximum quality and quantity of fruit on growth made the previous year.

One-year-old wood is pale green, two-year-old wood is grey and older wood is black. Every winter you should routinely cut back the old stems and remove any one-year-old growth that is too thin.

Newly planted stock must be cut back hard to encourage new basal shoots.

When pruning blackcurrants, you should cut out any old, black woody stems to encourage newer, more productive growth.

Pruning blackcurrants

Although old bushes will produce a modicum of fruit, the most productive canes are two years old. For maximum productivity, you should encourage new growth with ample organic fertiliser and systematically remove old wood.

The age of the wood can readily be recognised by the colour of the stems. New wood is pale green and two-year-old wood is grey, while older, non-productive wood is black (see illustration).

Some recommended blackcurrants

Early	Boskoop Giant
	Laxton's Giant
	Tsema
Mid-season	Ben Lomond
	Ben More
	Blackdown
	Blacksmith
	Seabrook's Black
Late	Amos Black
	Baldwin
	Ben Sarek
	Ben Tirran

Red- and whitecurrants
Ribes rubrum cultivars

Both these currants should be cultivated in the same fashion, as whitecurrants are simply a colour variant of the red.

These plants are generally grown as bushes, although fans and cordons are not uncommon. Redcurrants will tolerate warmer conditions than their black cousins. The fruit is borne on spurs produced by cutting back side-shoots. Tip pruning of main branches is recommended.

Thanks to good pruning, this redcurrant bush carries a bumper crop.

Pruning redcurrants

The bushes should be grown so as to develop an open structure. They fruit on spurs produced by pruning back lateral growths and shortening young shoots in late winter. The main branches should also be tipped back at the same time.

Recommended redcurrants

Early	Jonkheervan Tets
	Laxton's No. 1
Mid-season	Red Lake
	Random
	Stanza

Recommended whitecurrants

Early	none
Mid-season	White Dutch
	White Grape
	White Versailles

Some recommended gooseberries

Early	Broom Girl
	Golden Drop
	May Duke
Mid-season	Bedford Red
	Careless
	Crown Bob
	Langley Gage
	Leveller
	Whitesmith
Late	Captivator
	Lancashire Lad
	London
	Lord Derby
	White Lion

An open-structured gooseberry bush will produce a better harvest.

Gooseberries
Ribes uva-crispa cultivars

The cultivars available to the gardener will produce either culinary fruit or dessert fruit in a variety of yellow, red, white and green. Gooseberries are normally cultivated as a bush, though they can also be trained as a standard, a cordon or a fan.

Young plants should be systematically thinned to produce an open-centred bush. Regular pruning involves the removal of low-growing and crowded shoots. Spur pruning is achieved by cutting back all side-shoots to within 3 in (8 cm) of the main stem. Tip pruning will control the size of the plant.

Pruning gooseberries

Gooseberries are remarkably similar to redcurrants as regards the appropriate methods of cultivation and pruning. Cutting back spur growths will encourage higher productivity, while removal of overcrowded shoots will further improve the harvest.

The old canes from summer-fruiting raspberries should be removed once harvesting is over.

Raspberries
Rubus idaeus cultivars

This popular fruit enjoys the cooler, damper climate of Scotland, but will in fact tolerate most temperate climates.

Raspberries are of two types: the summer-fruiting varieties, which produce a heavy crop in mid-summer, and the autumn-fruiting raspberries, which begin fruiting in early autumn and only finish with the first frosts.

Summer-fruiting raspberries must be cut down to ground level immediately after harvesting so as to enable young canes to become established for fruit

Recommended raspberries

Summer-fruiting		Autumn-fruiting
Early	Delight	
	Glencoe	Autumn Bliss
	Glen Moy	Heritage
	Malling Promise	September
	Southland	Zeva
	Sumner	
Mid-season	Glen Prosen	
	Malling Jewel	
	Orion	
Late	Augusta	
	Leo	
	Malling Admiral	
	Malling Joy	

It's important know whether your raspberries are a summer-fruiting or an autumn-fruiting variety. This one — Glen Moy — is an early summer-fruiting variety.

bearing the following season. The autumn-fruiting varieties should generally be cut down hard at the end of the winter; the new canes will develop sufficiently to bear fruit the following autumn.

Pruning raspberries

The biggest single problem when cultivating and pruning raspberries is that of differentiating between summer-fruiting and autumn-fruiting varieties. The list of recommended varieties on the preceding page will provide some assistance in this.

Summer-fruiting raspberries

These should be pruned in the late summer after you have finished harvesting (right): cut back the old fruiting canes that have already borne fruit; allow the new canes to develop, then tie them back. They may need tipping back the following spring.

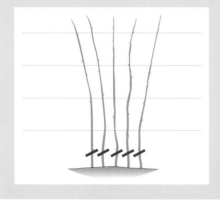

Autumn-fruiting raspberries

Remove all the canes in the late winter and early spring (left). This will encourage the growth of young shoots, which will flower and then fruit in the autumn.

Grapes
Vitis vinifera cultivars

Grape vines are extremely tolerant of some of the excesses of a temperate climate, although a hot, dry summer is needed to enable the fruits to ripen. The other primary requirement is very well-drained soil. (For greenhouse-grown grapes, see page 45.)

A hot, dry summer with plenty of sunshine is needed to produce a harvest as rich as this one.

Pruning grape vines

Grape vines produce fruit on one-year-old stems, and need to be cut back immediately after harvesting. On established plants, where there is an opportunity to control the harvest, young shoots must be encouraged to develop, but once the fruit starts to form they should be controlled by cutting back. Growth on young vines must be cut back and tied in the autumn.

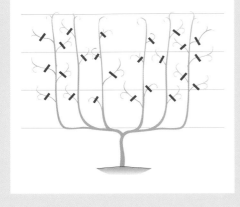

Single cordons (above) can be controlled by cutting back lateral growths in the winter.

Multiple cordons (left) are controlled by cutting back fruit-bearing laterals immediately after fruit set. As the season progresses, the leaves must be thinned to permit the maximum of sunlight to penetrate to the fruit.

Some recommended grapes

There is a tremendous range of grape varieties available, but your choice will be restricted to those able to withstand the cool summers associated with the British climate:

Black Hamburgh will be very productive in a warm situation outdoors, or as a dessert variety in a cold greenhouse.

Riesling Sylvaner is the most successful variety in terms of wine production.

Seyve Villard is also a reliable cropper — it is easy to grow and is acceptable as a dessert fruit.

The vines produce fruit on the current season's growth, but before that it is imperative for them to develop a framework or basic structure. Young plants may be encouraged to grow as single cordons or as a multiple, but in either case there should be an emphasis on strong growth and the production of the basic fabric, which should then produce fruit-bearing growth after about three years.

Here is the recommended procedure:

• In the first winter, cut back the leader by two-thirds, eliminating any secondary side-shoots.

• The following summer, tie in the principal leader and pinch back any laterals.

• The following winter, cut back the leader by one-third, and remove any lateral growths.

• Repeat this procedure over the subsequent summer and

43

winter, by which time a strong vine will have developed.

- Fruiting spurs will develop — you should allow one bunch per stem, which must be cut back to about four leaves after fruit set.

Dessert grapes will benefit from growing on a warm wall, where reflected heat will help the fruit to ripen more effectively.

Wine grapes are usually harvested in mid-autumn; if you thin the leaves, this will improve ripening by enabling a maximum of light to reach the fruit.

Right *A citrus plant growing in a pot in a conservatory can be moved outdoors in the summer.*

Below *A grape vine growing on a wall will benefit greatly from the warmth and shelter it provides.*

Greenhouse fruits

Growing exotic fruits in a conservatory or greenhouse is not very popular these days. However, it can be extremely satisfying to grow fruit trees that will benefit from protection, particularly during the winter months.

Citrus fruits

These plants will grow very well in large pots and can be developed into pleasing small shrubs up to about 4 ft (1.25 m) tall. The usual practice is to cultivate them as greenhouse plants that can be put outside during the warmer summer months.

Citrus plants require virtually no pruning other than cutting back any very strong growth to develop a rounded shrub.

As evergreens they make a valuable visual contribution to the landscape of a conservatory. The fruits produced in these situations are a bonus.

The common Valencia orange and the clementine (mandarin) can both be grown from seed.

Peaches

A common practice in the UK is to grow peaches under glass or as fan-trained plants. They can usually be obtained from the nursery with the rudiments of an outline, and can then be encouraged to develop into highly productive plants with a maximum span of 8 ft (2.5 m). You can achieve this by allowing only the straight leaders to develop and cutting out all the thin lateral spurs or pinching back young buds in summer.

Grapes

Dessert grapes, usually greenhouse-grown black varieties, have a fantastic flavour. You should first allow the plant to develop as a cordon for three years, cutting back all lateral growths to three or four leaves. Once a good fabric has been established, you can then allow fruit to develop, with just one bunch per spur. You should cut back all spurs in the early winter, as they will bleed badly if you leave them too late.

A conservatory vine can yield a rich harvest of sweet-tasting grapes.

Ornamental trees

There is an enormous variety of ornamental trees available, whether to enhance the landscape of large plantings or to contribute to the intimacy of a small garden.

The majority of our native trees and naturalised introductions require very little in the way of maintenance. They generally demand the attention of a saw only on rare occasions, such as when there has been damage from storms or passing vehicles, or from the over-enthusiastic attention of fellow human beings. Occasionally a tree has to be dissuaded from

obscuring natural light, but such a situation has usually been created by thoughtless planting in the first place.

Should branches be damaged by natural causes such as lightning or high winds, it is fool-hardy to embark on major sawing operations without being very well equipped with safety harness, chainsaws etc. In such situations it is far better to employ the skills of professional tree surgeons.

Garden trees

When growing trees in the garden, it is important to control the enthusiasm with which some decorative trees try to take over. In such situations some

A Judas tree (Cercis siliquastrum)

An ornamental cherry in blossom is a glorious sight.

they demand expensive anchoring, which has to be maintained for several years or more. Leaf fall can also be a problem in some gardens, obstructing drainage and smothering lawns and other garden plants.

Nevertheless there is a whole range of easy-to-maintain ornamental trees which can give immense colour and variety to a garden during all the seasons of the year.

Some trees for the smaller garden

The species and cultivars listed in the table below will serve a variety of tastes, and none of them require too much in the way of maintenance.

Developed as half or full standards, they require little pruning other than the elimination of crossed branches and broken stems. Many of these, however, will bleed profusely if you cut them back too late, so it is advisable to complete such 'surgery' by the end of January.

judicious cutting-back may be called for.

If you are an enthusiast for 'greening the planet', then you would be wise to think carefully before planting a tree in a small garden. You should first consider the eventual height and breadth of a mature specimen and the implications of potential overcrowding.

Two major factors to consider are the cost of maintenance and the impact of the tree on its immediate environment. Many trees, for example, have a surface rooting system, which may cause considerable damage to the drains and the footings of buildings, not to mention the constant cost of staking. Many *Crataegus* (hawthorns) are notorious for their instability;

Some trees for the smaller garden

Species/variety	Common name/notable features
Acer capillipes	Smoke-barked maple
Amelanchier lamarckii	Tree or shrub with white flowers and bright autumn colours
Catalpa bignonioides 'Aurea'	Indian bean tree
Cercis siliquastrum	Judas tree
Cornus kousa	A dogwood
Crataegus laevigata 'Paul's Scarlet'	A hawthorn cultivar
Laburnum × waterii 'Vossi Brilliant'	Voss's laburnum — decked with chains of yellow flowers
Magnolia × loebneri 'Merrill'	Lilac-pink flowers
Malus 'Dartmouth'	A crab apple
Melia azedarach	Bead tree, Persian lilac
Prunus cultivars	Flowering cherries
Pyrus calleryana 'Chanticlear'	An ornamental pear
Sorbus aria	Whitebeam
Stewartii pseudocamellia	Pretty bark and autumn foliage
Syringa	Lilac
Vitex agnus-castus	Chaste tree

Ornamental shrubs

Flowering shrubs can contribute so much to the garden. They may provide pretty flowers and coloured foliage throughout the growing season, followed by attractive fruits in the autumn, and in some instances by the luxury of coloured bark and stems in the winter.

Given the wide selection of plants available, their treatment in terms of cutting back, pruning and general control will vary enormously. They can, however, be roughly divided into groups, each of which shares similar methods of culture:

1 Deciduous shrubs that need minimal pruning.

2 Deciduous shrubs that should be pruned in the spring.

3 Shrubs that should be pruned in summer after flowering.

4 Evergreen shrubs that tolerate severe pruning.

5 Evergreen shrubs that require minimal pruning.

6 Shrubs such as dogwoods that will enhance the garden if they are either pollarded or coppiced (these are dealt with in the section on coppicing on pages 70-71).

Above *Lilac (Syringa) is justifiably popular for its glorious display of blooms — it normally requires only minimal pruning in the summer after flowering has finished.*

Left *Pruning a specimen of Philadelphus coronarius 'Aureus' — this again should be done in the summer after flowering.*

Deciduous shrubs that need minimal pruning

All the shrubs in the table to the right are natural growers that require very little maintenance. Should branches have to be trimmed at any stage, this is best done in the winter to avoid excessive bleeding.

Deciduous shrubs that should be pruned in spring

These are all shrubs which flower on the current season's growth. If a plant has been neglected, you should cut out very old wood to begin with, and then seasonally reduce to younger, fresher and more productive fabric.

Aloysia (lemon verbena)
Buddleia davidii (butterfly bush)
Ceanothus 'Autumnal Blue'
Ceratostigma willmottianum
Cotinus (smoke tree)
Fuchsia (hardy cultivars)
Hibiscus syriacus
Hydrangea
Hypericum
Indigofera
Lavatera (tree mallow)
Perovskia
Sorbaria
Spiraea douglasii
Tamarix (tamarisk)
Zauschneria

Shrubs that should be pruned in summer after flowering

Buddleia alternifolia
Chaenomeles (flowering quince)
Cotoneaster
Deutzia
Dipelta
Exochorda
Holodiscus
Jasminum humile (yellow jasmine)
Kolkwitzia
Magnolia × *soulangeana*
Magnolia stellata
Philadelphus
Photinia villosa
Ribes sanguineum (flowering currant)
Spiraea × *arguta* (bridal wreath)
Spiraea prunifolia
Spiraea thunbergii
Stephanandra
Syringa (lilac)
Viburnum
Weigela

Amelanchier (serviceberry)
Chimonanthus (wintersweet)
Corylopsis
Cytisus (broom)
Decaisnea
Euonomus europaeus (spindle tree)
Hamamelis (witch hazel)
Genista (broom)
Poncirus (Japanese bitter orange)
Potentilla (shrub forms)
Salix (ornamental willows)
Syringa (lilac)

Removing the old wood from a badly neglected butterfly bush

Evergreen shrubs that will tolerate severe pruning

Some evergreens can occasionally become too big for the garden, and you may find you need to cut back the invasive offenders very hard. In some instances, however, this can have fatal consequences, and you would be well advised to know this before choosing such a plant in the first place.

Here, then, is a list of those evergreen shrubs that can be expected to withstand the pressures of severe pruning should this be required at any stage:

> *Aucuba*
> *Berberis darwinii*
> *Buxus* (box)
> *Choisya ternata* (Mexican orange blossom)
> *Escallonia* 'Donard Seedling'
> *Euonymous fortunei*
> *Ligustrum japonicum* (Japanese privet)
> *Phillyrea*
> *Prunus lusitanica* (Portuguese laurel)
> *Santolina*
> *Sarcococca humilis*
> *Taxus* (yew)
> *Viburnum tinus* (laurustinus)
> *Rhododendron ponticum*

Winter jasmine (Jasminum nudiflorum) is unusual in producing flowers while still bare of foliage. Like any climber that flowers on the previous season's growth, it should be pruned when flowering is over.

Evergreen shrubs that only require minimal pruning

The majority of evergreens are extremely hardy and require very little maintenance.

If anything the reverse is true and great damage can be done by lopping off leaders to restrain growth. There is nothing uglier than a plant that has been foreshortened.

Sometimes, however, a very young or newly planted shrub can produce a rogue branch that becomes obtrusive and upsets the equilibrium of the young plant. In such cases a little judicious cutting-back will encourage conformity.

Here is a list of those plants for which light pruning only is required (all of them are in fact conifers):

> *Chamaecyparis obtusa* 'Nana Aurea'
> *Juniperus scopulorum* 'Skyrocket'
> *Juniperus squamata* 'Blue Star'
> *Pinus sylvestris* 'Gold Coin'
> *Thuja orientalis* 'Aurea Nana'

Ornamental climbers

The majority of climbers will benefit from being encouraged to cover walls, fences etc. by the simple process of formative pruning, thereby retaining strong shoots to establish a good basic structure. Eventually branches will have to be trained in a horizontal mode, which will encourage a greater production of flowers.

Climbers can be roughly divided into two groups in terms of the pruning required:

1 those that flower on the previous season's growth;

2 those that flower on the current season's growth.

In practice this means that if wood is removed during the winter from plants in the first category such as *Actinidia*, *Clematis montana* or *Wisteria*, they will be deprived of flowers

Japonica (Chaenomeles japonica) is one of our most popular climbers on account of its beautiful flowers.

the following summer. The table below left gives a general indication of which climbers belong to each of the two groups. *Clematis* includes plants in both categories, so is dealt with separately on page 53.

Ornamental climbers that flower on the previous season's growth

Actinidia	*Jasminum*	*Solandra maxima*
Chaenomeles	*Pileostegia*	*Strongylodon*
Hydrangea	*Schizophragma*	*Wisteria*

Ornamental climbers that flower on the current season's growth

Bignonia	*Ipomoea*	*Polygonum aubertii*
Campsis	*Mandevilla*	*Thunbergia*
Clianthus	*Plumbago*	

Some popular climbers

There are some popular climbers which merit special mention at this point:

Japonica
Chaenomeles japonica

On established trained plants on fences and walls, you should cut back side-shoots after flowering has finished, and shorten outgrowing laterals as they develop.

Bougainvillea
Bougainvillea cultivars

The bougainvillea is not a climber that is normally associated with the UK, but its great beauty is making it ever more popular as a plant for warm microclimates, cold greenhouses and conservatories.

The plant must be encouraged to grow. If any wood has to be removed, this should be done after flowering, or else early in the spring to control rampant growth.

Wisteria
Wisteria cultivars

Wisterias are reluctant to flower if they are allowed to develop excessive amounts of leafy material.

Towards the end of the summer you should cut back any short stems carrying an excess of foliage, and reduce longer branches to short spurs.

In the winter you should cut back these summer spurs to about two or three buds. No wood should be removed on strong growths that will enhance the size of the plant; you should tie these back in a horizontal position if possible.

Wisteria looks particularly good trained across the wall of a house, as these two pictures show.

Pruning wisteria

The members of the genus *Wisteria* show a marked reluctance to flower if they are not properly pruned, and the abundance of annual growth must therefore be curtailed.

This can be achieved by first cutting back in the late summer, reducing long shoots to about 6 in (15 cm), and restricting or even eliminating the short, leafy shoots.

In the winter (see illustration) any shoots that have already been reduced in the summer should be further shortened. However, if the plant is to be extended, then some stems may be left and tied in.

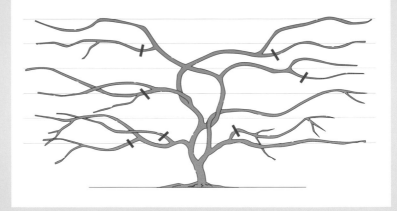

Clematis
Clematis species and cultivars

Clematis are generally divided into three groups according to their period of flowering; this also affects their pruning:

Group 1 consists of the early-flowering species, and the Alpina, Macropetala and Montana groups of cultivars, which flower directly on the previous season's stems.

Group 2 are the early large-flowered cultivars, which bloom on short stems of the current season's growth.

Group 3 are the late-flowering species, the late large-flowered cultivars and the herbaceous types.

All clematis must be cut back when newly planted down to about 12 in (30 cm) in their first spring to encourage a plentiful supply of wood from the base.

After that, plants in **Group 1** require very little pruning. Any excessive growth can be

With large-flowered clematis you need to know whether they belong to Group 2 or Group 3 for the purposes of pruning.

reduced in the autumn, though this will reduce flowering wood the following spring.

Group 2 plants must be cut back in early spring before new

Some recommended clematis

Group 1 Early-flowering clematis	Group 2 Early large-flowered cultivars	Group 3 Late-flowering clematis: species	cultivars
Clematis alpina	Barbara Jackman	*C. florida*	Comtesse de Bouchard
C. armandii	Daniel Deronda	*C. tangutica*	Earnest Markham
C. cirrhosa	Duchess of Edinburgh	*C. viticella*	Hagley Hybrid
C. macropetala	Lasurstern		Jackmanii
C. montana	Mme Le Coultre		Ville de Lyon
	Nelly Moser		
	The President		

growth appears. Any weak or damaged stems may also be removed at this time.

Members of **Group 3** should also be cut back in the spring but very much harder — i.e. to about 12 in (30 cm) from ground level.

Clematis tangutica is one of the late-flowering species, and needs to be pruned hard to keep it under some kind of control.

Pruning clematis

Group 1: Early-flowering clematis
These are generally allowed to grow naturally, particularly the species. If they have to be controlled, then this should be done immediately after flowering (see right), when some of the old wood can be eliminated so as to prevent overcrowding.

Group 2: Early large-flowered cultivars
The flowers form on short stems of the current season's growth. Old flowering wood and spindly growth is usually removed in the spring (see left).

Group 3: Late-flowering clematis
These plants generally flower on the current season's growth. This necessitates heavy pruning in the spring (see right), removing all the previous year's wood down to about 1 ft (30 cm).

Pruning roses

There was an old gardening maxim which, roughly interpreted, meant that to obtain good roses you had to get your enemy to prune them. The general implication was that the harder they were treated, the greater the excellence and quality of the bloom.

Fortunately we live in a more enlightened age. The development of the rose, and its popularity, has moved on from the dark ages so that it has become the world's favourite garden plant. Nowadays, although it might be an exaggeration to say that the modern rose thrives on neglect, there is certainly not the propensity to cut everything down to ground level.

The simplest method of discussing the pruning of roses is to consider each category of rose according to its place in the history of the genus *Rosa*.

Many wild roses are prized for their hips as much as for their flowers. This can certainly be said for Rosa moyesii 'Geranium', *although its flowers are equally attractive.*

Like most wild rose types, Rosa xanthina 'Canary Bird' *should normally be left unpruned.*

Species roses (wild roses)

There are probably some 120–130 species roses to be found in the Northern Hemisphere, many of which make a valuable contribution to the garden. Although principally grown for their abundance of flowers and harvest of spectacular hips, they include some roses that are grown for the quality and colour of their foliage.

These plants are all wild roses that have been discovered in various temperate regions of the world. They are now accepted as providing a beautiful addition to borders and natural plantings.

Species roses very rarely if ever require pruning. On the contrary, any manipulation of their natural growth tends to create some extremely ugly plant shapes. Occasionally,

though, a stem needs removing in order to allow more light into the base of the tree. On such occasions the services of a handsaw become imperative.

Rosa xanthina *'Canary Bird'* really lives up to its name, with a magnificent display of canary-yellow blooms.

Some popular wild roses

Species/variety	Valuable features
Rosa ecae 'Helen Knight'	flowers
R. glauca syn. *R. rubrifolia*	foliage and hips
R. hugonis	flowers and foliage
R. macrophylla	hips
R. moyesii 'Geranium'	flowers and hips
R. multiflora	flowers
R. pomifera	flowers and hips
R. primula	flowers and scented foliage
R. rubiginosa (sweetbriar)	scented foliage
R. sericea pteracantha	foliage
R. souliana	foliage
R. sweginzowii	hips
R. xanthina 'Canary Bird'	flowers

Pruning wild roses

Virtually all wild roses that are gardenworthy must be allowed to develop naturally. The foreshortening of any stems will produce ugly plants and an unnatural silhouette. They should never be dead-headed, as the majority produce a fantastic show of hips.

Occasionally there may be an accumulation of old, twiggy stems. These are best removed in the early winter at ground level, using a light handsaw. You should only ever remove very old, non-productive wood (black in illustration). Never shorten young, virile stems.

Rosa Mundi, like other summer-flowering old garden roses, benefits from being pruned after flowering.

A selection of popular summer-flowering old garden roses

Albas
Great Maiden's Blush
Königin von Dänemark
Mme Plantier

Centifolias
Fantin-Latour
Robert le Diable
Tour de Malakoff

Damask roses
Kazanlik
Mme Hardy
York and Lancs

Gallicas
Complicata
Cardinal de Richelieu
Charles de Mills
Tuscany Superb
Versicolor

Moss roses
Blanche Moreau
Common Moss
Nuits de Young
Striped Moss
William Lobb

Old garden roses

These can be conveniently divided into two distinct categories: summer-flowering and recurrent-flowering.

Summer-flowering old garden roses

As their title implies, this group of roses enjoys a magnificent flush of flower in early to mid-summer. Historically speaking, they constitute the European contribution to the development of the rose. Many varieties have romantic links with history, having names evocative of the 16th, 17th and 18th centuries.

The important point to remember is that all these roses flower on wood made the previous year. Any pruning must therefore be done immediately after flowering — usually towards the end of July — which in effect means summer pruning. This

Summer-flowering old garden roses

This group includes the damasks and centifolias. New young stems should always be encouraged, as this type of rose produces the finest flower on wood made the previous year.

Quite the most satisfactory method of encouraging new wood is heavy dead-heading immediately after flowering, removing as much as 2-3 ft (60–90 cm) of growth.

Occasionally in the winter one or two old stems can be removed at ground level.

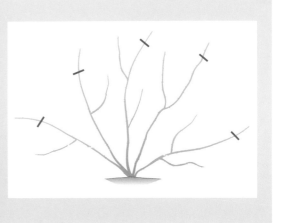

long-forgotten art will in fact encourage these plants to produce an abundance of new wood, which will yield high-quality blooms the following season.

Moss roses are possibly an exception to this procedure. They are not normally very productive of much wood and usually only require light dead-heading.

Hybrid sweetbriars too are not normally cut back, as most of them produce a good crop of bright red hips in the autumn.

William Lobb is one of the moss roses, and therefore needs only light dead-heading.

Buff Beauty is one of the hybrid musks.

Louise Odier — a bourbon rose

Rosa rugosa rubra

Recurrent-flowering old garden roses

These old garden roses were the precursors of the modern garden varieties. They are divided into the following categories:

- China roses
- tea roses
- noisettes
- bourbons
- hybrid perpetuals
- hybrid musks
- Rugosas

Chinas, teas and noisettes

A wide variety of rose types, most of which grow into bushes or small shrubs, although one or two are climbers. They require vigorous dead-heading as the blooms age so as to encourage a continuity of flower. In early spring remove any old or dead branches; some may have frosted wood, as they are not particularly hardy. But formative pruning to control their shape and size is more important than rigorously cutting them back.

Bourbons

The bourbons are all vigorous shrubs — highly evocative of the Victorian era. They can also be used in abundance as cut flowers.

These roses require careful dead-heading in the summer to give a good shape to the plant and encourage good autumn flowering.

In the springtime you should cut out any old, dead wood and carry out a certain amount of formative pruning.

Hybrid perpetuals

Most of these roses are large, coarse plants, in many instances with very big blooms. They should be dead-headed only lightly to allow them to develop into medium-sized shrubs. A big mistake is to cut them back very hard in the spring. This will produce gigantic blooms but will also encourage tall, ugly stems, which are not a pretty sight.

Hybrid musks

These very pretty, medium-sized plants will take two or three years to develop into beautiful shrubs. They benefit greatly from being dead-headed immediately after flowering in July. This encourages an abundance of autumn colour. In spring you should only remove old flowering wood, and allow the plants to grow into shrubs 5 ft (1.5 m) wide by 5 ft (1.5 m) tall.

Rugosas

The wild ancestor, *Rosa rugosa*, is a species of rose characterised by very thorny stems and large, luxuriant leathery leaves; many

A selection of popular recurrent-flowering old garden roses

China roses
Cécile Brunner
Mutabilis
Old Blush

Tea roses
Gloire de Dijon
Lady Hillingdon
Niphetos

Noisettes
Mme Alfred Carrière
Maréchal Niel
William Allen Richardson

Bourbons
Honorine de Brabant
La Reine Victoria
Mme Isaac Pereire
Zéphirine Drouhin

Hybrid perpetuals
Ferdinand Pichard
Frau Karl Druschki
Paul Neyron
Roger Lambelin

Hybrid musks
Buff Beauty
Cornelia
Penelope
Prosperity

Rugosas
Blanc Double de Coubert
Frau Dagmar Hastrupp
Kordes Robusta
Roserie de l'Haÿ
Rosa rugosa alba
R. rugosa rubra

varieties also produce large, round hips in the autumn. Most are ideal as hedging material or large specimen shrubs.

Rugosas require virtually no pruning. On the contrary, to cut back their stems produces very ugly growth. No dead-heading

is needed. Occasionally some of the bigger plants get thin and straggly. The remedy then is to cut them back to about 12 in (30 cm), usually with a saw, at the beginning of January. Young wood will quickly develop into a rejuvenated plant structure.

Recurrent-flowering old garden roses

The immediate predecessors of the modern rose, these plants should in general be heavily dead-headed after the first flush of flower, then lightly pruned the following spring with the accent on achieving a good shape to the plant.

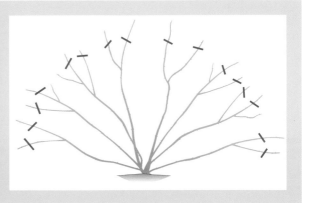

Climbing and rambling roses

This group can again be divided into summer-flowering and recurrent-flowering forms.

Summer-flowering climbers and ramblers

This section comprises the majority of the older ramblers and climbers, most of which share one common denominator: they only flower once in the summer. They therefore share an identity with many other

Rambling Rector is such a vigorous old rambler that it will climb up trees to great heights with little aid or encouragement.

A selection of popular summer-flowering climbers and ramblers

Albéric Barbier	Maigold
Albertine	Masquerade
Climbing Cécile Brunner	Paul's Scarlet
Crimson Glory	Rambling Rector
Crimson Shower	*Rosa longicuspis*
Dorothy Perkins	Spek's Yellow
François Juranville	The Garland
Iceberg	Wedding Day
Kiftsgate	

shrubs and climbers in that they flower on wood made the previous season.

Consequently, these roses require the greatest attention in the autumn. The procedure is to tie in new wood and cut back as much old wood as possible, while at the same time maintaining a good outline fabric to the plant. A slow-growing variety should be allowed to retain as much wood as possible, whereas some of the very vigorous

old ramblers can be reduced considerably.

Immediately after flowering, all roses in this range will benefit from dead-heading, and all young wood as it develops must be tied in to avoid damage in windy conditions.

Some of the very vigorous ramblers can be persuaded to climb into trees so as to produce a remarkable show of blooms at considerable heights. These need no cutting-back at all and will thrive without any aid apart from annual feeding.

Careful treatment is needed — reducing old flowering wood and rearranging new growth — to create a rose arch such as this one.

Summer-flowering ramblers and climbers

Although climbers in this category must be allowed to develop good permanent structures, the secret of producing large swathes of colour is to encourage fresh new canes immediately after bloom has faded. As the new growth develops, tie it in to prevent wind damage. Then in autumn reduce the old flowering wood and rearrange the new stems to achieve a good distribution of potential flowering wood.

Recurrent-flowering climbers and ramblers

These roses are relatively recent in the history and development of the rose. Indeed, they were almost unheard-of until after 1950. They are equally suitable for walls and pergolas, and if well maintained they have the potential to flower well into the autumn.

Because of their potential to flower so effusively, these climbers do not produce the same long climbing stems as their summer cousins do; they have to build up their total structure in a more pedestrian

Compassion is a recurrent-flowering climber that requires little maintenance other than some judicious trimming and dead-heading.

fashion. In effect this means that, apart from dead-heading during the flowering season, they require no other maintenance apart from removing any remaining dead-heads in the spring together with some of the ageing wood.

A selection of modern recurrent-flowering climbers and ramblers

Compassion	Morning Jewel
Dublin Bay	Pink Perpétue
Golden Showers	Schoolgirl
Handel	The New Dawn
Laura Ford	Warm Welcome
Mme A. Carrière	Zéphirine Drouhin

Recurrent-flowering ramblers and climbers

Because of their propensity to produce a lot of flower on climbing wood, these roses demand judicious trimming to allow the plant to develop properly in a process that may take up to two or three years.

Heavy dead-heading is the norm, though an ageing stem may occasionally be removed to encourage rejuvenation.

An established modern climber requires heavy dead-heading, and tying back to prevent wind damage.

One advantageous method of relocating branches (see right) is to bend them into an **arching mode**. This encourages a greater production of flower over the whole plant, and prevents climbers especially from going bare at the bottom.

Floribunda and hybrid tea bush roses

While some catalogues may list these two types as cluster-flowered and large-flowered respectively, there is a marked reluctance to adopt these new descriptions. However, experts are unanimous in grouping these two categories together for the purposes of describing pruning.

Gardeners nowadays are no longer determined to reduce them all down to stumps every spring — or at least not unless they want to produce very large exhibition blooms.

Modern practice makes for a much simpler exercise:

1 Mentally divide a mature bush into thirds towards the end of the growing season.

2 About the end of October, reduce the bush by one-third, principally to reduce wind damage in the winter gales.

3 In the spring, remove the second third of the plant — i.e. reduce the remaining part of the bush by about 50 percent.

Gardeners no longer insist on removing all the remaining twiggy growth — although it is imperative to cut out any old and decaying stumps. Recent research suggests that these small stems and their associated leaf structure make a valuable

Elina — a hybrid tea

A selection of modern bush roses

Floribundas	Hybrid teas
Ainsley Dickson	Alec's Red
Amber Queen	Elina
Anna Livia	Fragrant Cloud
Arthur Bell	Just Joey
Iceberg	Pascali
Korresia	Paul Shirville
Margaret Merril	Peace
Matangi	Royal William
The Times Rose	Savoy Hotel
Trumpeter	Silver Jubilee

contribution to the quality of the flower. Meticulous dead-heading during the summer will encourage a continuity of flower.

Royal William is one of several hybrid tea roses that can be developed as a shrub.

Floribundas and hybrid teas

Modern practice recommends the retention of as much wood as possible commensurate with maintaining a healthy plant.

In the autumn, when the first frosts have begun, cut down your bush roses by about one-third to reduce the potential wind damage.

In the early spring, cut down a further third of the plant (i.e. half of what remains) and remove any ageing stumps; this may require a light saw.

Some floribundas and hybrid teas that can be developed into shrubs

Alexander
Iceberg
Keepsake
Many Happy Returns
Mountbatten
Peace
Royal William
Southampton
Tango
Troika

Tango — a floribunda that can be grown as a shrub

Developing floribundas and hybrid teas as shrubs

Developing a modern bush as a shrub is effectively a return to the natural form. Roses were, after all, originally shrubs. Varieties that are naturally vigorous but bushy can be persuaded into large shrubs by light pruning. Reducing a plant by about one-third annually in late autumn is more than sufficient.

Modern shrub roses can be dealt with in a similar fashion.

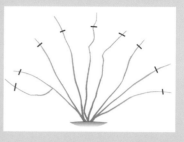

Modern bush roses make big shrubs

Further research has revealed that many modern hybrid teas and floribundas can be developed into quite large shrubs. This can be achieved by pruning very lightly in the spring, allowing them to grow into shrubs 6–7 ft (about 2 m) tall.

Modern shrub roses

There are many varieties of rose whose vigour merits them a separate division. Although usually described as modern shrubs, collectively they can most conveniently be described as 'floribundas that are not pruned'. Apart from dead-heading in the summer, these roses thrive with little mainte-nance other than pruning to shape in the spring.

Ballerina is one of the modern shrub roses, which require little pruning apart from shaping in the spring.

Nevada — a vigorous shrub rose

Some modern shrub roses

Ballerina
Bonica
Fred Loads
Graham Thomas
Golden Wings
Mary Rose
Nevada
Sally Holmes
The Fairy
Yesterday

Patio roses and miniatures

Bred specifically for the modern trend towards small gardens, patio roses can be described as low-growing floribundas — though with the proviso that if bred true to their original concept they should have miniature blooms and foliage.

Patio roses usually grow to about 2–3 ft (30–90 cm) in height. They should receive precisely the same treatment as other bush roses, being generally reduced by two-thirds in the spring.

Patio roses and miniatures

This modern form of rose is ideal for small gardens, patios and containers. Plants should be reduced by about a half in early spring, and the accumulation of dead wood at the base should also be cut out.

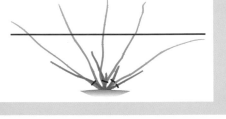

Miniature roses, which are even smaller, should be cut down in similar proportions.

Sweet Magic — ideal for the small garden

A selection of patio and miniature roses

Patios	Miniatures
Gentle Touch	Darling Flame
Little Bo-peep	Magic Carousel
Pretty Polly	Orange Sunblaze
Regensburg	Red Ace
Sweet Dream	Starina
Top Marks	

Some ground-cover roses

Large	Small
Chilterns	Flower Carpet
Ferdy	Gwent
Pheasant	Hertfordshire
Pink Bells	Northamptonshire
Red Blanket	Nozomi
Red Max Graf	Snow Carpet
Smarty	Suffolk
Tall Story	Surrey

Above *Suffolk is one of the small ground-cover roses.*

Right *Pheasant makes an attractive border rose.*

Ground-cover roses

These plants were originally conceived as a type of rose to give variety and colour to the choice of plants recommended for small and large landscaping projects. They have now become popular in many smaller gardens, and have added a new dimension to the adaptability of the rose.

As ground-cover roses are naturally spreading plants, they do not require the same manipulations as their bigger cousins. On the contrary, they do not require any pruning whatsoever.

A tidy-minded gardener might want to dead-head them, but this could be a mistake with some varieties, as many of them produce an attractive harvest of small, round hips.

Ground-cover roses

By definition, this type of modern plant should not require any regular pruning. These environmentally friendly roses have been bred to thrive with very little maintenance. If they have to be constrained, then quite the most efficient method is to trim them with garden shears.

Horticultural practices associated with pruning

Topiary

The practice of training and shaping trees and shrubs has been popular for many centuries. Topiary designs may range from simple architectural forms to elaborate bird and animal figures. They have lent great distinction to many gardens and given much pleasure to gardeners.

For topiary to be successful, you must be careful to choose the most suitable plant material. The main criterion for this is dense pliable growth, usually small-leaved and capable of recovering quickly after trimming and cutting back.

There are six suitable subjects that meet these parameters:

- yew (*Taxus baccata*);

- box (*Buxus sempervirens*);

- holly (*Ilex aquifolium*);

- bay (*Laurus nobilis*);

- *Lonicera nitida* (a honey-suckle species).

In addition to these there are some ivies (*Hedera*) that can be persuaded and trained into simple forms of topiary.

Even the most modest of suburban gardens will be enhanced by the incorporation of just a few simple topiary designs.

Intricate designs will require some form of skeletal device — usually heavy chicken wire — to tie in and encourage young growth. The majority of topiary figures can be trimmed about twice a year. But you should not leave the last cutting too late, or else the young growths may be damaged by early frosts.

The greatest danger to these intricate plant forms is the weight of lying snow in the winter. You can avoid this to a certain extent by discouraging large horizontal surfaces where snow might accumulate. Otherwise the only really practical solution is physically removing great accumulations as and when they occur.

Right *Topiary is traditionally associated with the elaborate gardens on our great country estates.*

Developing a topiary figure

The more elaborate forms of topiary are developed by building an outline of chicken wire. They are then trained and clipped as the new growth emerges. More substantial erections are made by constructing a strong skeleton of angle iron. This not only provides a reliable guide, but also gives added support in snowy conditions.

Coppicing and pollarding

Trees and shrubs that if coppiced or pollarded will provide excellent winter colouring:

Acer pennsylvanicum (snake-bark maple)
Cornus alba 'Sibirica'
C. stolonifera 'Flaviramea
Corylus avellana (cobnut)
Eucalyptus dalrympleana (mountain gum)
E. gunnii (cider gum)
E. pauciflora (snow gum)
Populus × *canadensis* 'Serotina Aurea'
Salix alba 'Britzensis' (white willow)
S. a. 'Tristis' (golden weeping willow)
Tilia platyphyllos (broad-leaved lime)

Eucalyptus *makes an excellent subject for coppicing.*

Coppicing

With plants such as red-barked dogwood (*Cornus alba*), coppicing can be used to enhance the red colour of the bark in winter. The method is simple and very effective:

1 Take a well-established specimen of *Cornus alba*.

2 Cut back hard in the spring after the winter display of bark.

3 The foliage on the vigorous new shoots will later provide rich display of autumn colouring.

4 The following spring, cut the bright-red stems back again to encourage yet another flush of autumn and winter colour.

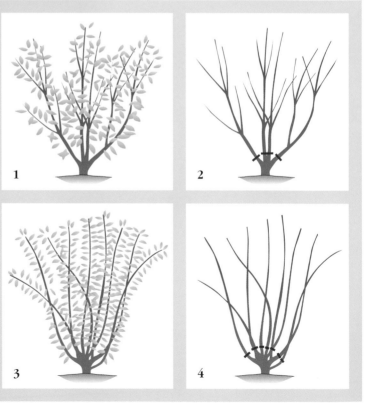

Coppicing

Coppicing is the regular cutting back of a tree or shrub virtually to ground level.

At one time this was a regular practice in country areas to encourage woody stems for the production of sheep hurdles (hazel) and basketwork (willow). It is now enjoying something of a revival.

In the ornamental garden you can create many beautiful and interesting colour formations by using this technique, and with many shrubs such as dogwoods (*Cornus*) you can bring out the natural colour.

Pollarding

Pollarding is a simple exercise. Trees are allowed to grow to about 6 ft (2 m), and then pruned back to this height every two or three years, thus developing into a mass of colourful shoots. Although this practice is principally associated with rural scenes of willows on riverbanks, there are many other plants that will respond well to this method of arboriculture.

This is not, however, to be confused with the damage wrought by municipal authorities who resort to cutting back badly selected material merely to provide access for public transport.

Pleached trees

Pleached or plashed trees are standard or half-standard trees that have been planted in rows and their branches trained horizontally so as to create a

Pleaching

This technique is thought of as the epitome of excellence in the art of training or persuading trees to grow in a particular way. Pleaching is used to create whole avenues of greenery.

First a timber framework is built and growth is encouraged so as to form a horizontal fabric.

As new wood is produced, so it is trained in and cut back.

When a substantial fabric has developed, all laterals growing away from the tree are tied in or cut back, and given time the timber frame can be removed.

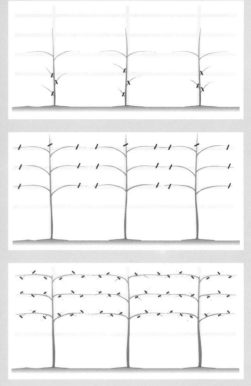

wall or walls of foliage when in leaf. Hornbeams and some varieties of lime are ideal for this purpose.

In order to construct such an 'avenue' it is vital to build a suitable wooden framework along which the branches can be encouraged to grow horizontally. Once this framework is firmly in place, stems growing

away from the framework should be cut back, while new horizontal stems are tied in. The wooden framework can then be dismantled once the pleached trees have become established.

The secret of success is to plant young trees that are producing pliable stems, and to maintain a rapid rate of growth by means of regular feeding.

Hedges and screens

There are very few gardens that do not possess a hedge of some kind. Such hedges may have a primarily functional or a mainly ornamental role. But whatever the position or status of the hedge, you must always bear in mind that like any other plant in the garden it must be regularly maintained by good husbandry and feeding.

Functional hedges or screens are usually evergreen, although this is not completely true, as deciduous genera such as *Carpinus* (hornbeam) and *Fagus* (beech) also make excellent screening material. Informal hedges are normally made up of decorative shrubs that can be persuaded to produce colourful boundaries.

The choice and position of hedges depends not only on personal taste but on various practical criteria, the most

Above *An avenue of pleached limes (see previous page)*

Below *An interesting combination of formal and informal hedges*

important factor being access for maintenance and trimming.

As a general rule, most hedges must be sheared about twice a year — once in late spring and once in early autumn. However, there are wide variations in the timing of this seasonal activity.

Some recommended subjects for hedging

Formal hedges

Evergreen

Box (*Buxus*)	Clip two or three times a year.
Lawson's cypress	Clip twice, in spring and early autumn.
Privet (*Ligustrum*)	Clip two or three times a year.
Lonicera nitida	Clip two or three times a year.
Yew (*Taxus*)	Clip usually at the beginning of August.

Deciduous

Berberis thunbergii	Clip in mid-summer.
Hornbeam (*Carpinus*)	Clip in mid to late summer.
Hawthorn (*Crataegus*)	Clip in mid to late summer.
Beech (*Fagus*)	Clip in mid to late summer.

Informal hedges

Evergreen

Berberis darwinii	Clip immediately after flowering.
Cotoneaster lacteus	Clip after fruiting.
Garrya elliptica	Clip after fruiting.
Pyracantha	Clip in late summer.

Deciduous

Berberis thunbergii	Clip after flowering.
Hawthorn (*Crataegus*)	Clip during the winter.
Rose cultivars	Thin out in the spring; do not cut back.

Hedges like these look very good, but require a tremendous amount of work to maintain, and some of them will be liable to damage from the weight of winter snow.

Whatever type of hedge you plant, it is imperative for it to be trimmed very precisely — a garden line is an essential tool for this purpose. A hedge with an uneven top looks quite dreadful and can detract from the total ambience of a garden.

Snow damage is the greatest problem, especially with evergreen hedges. The best solution is to minimise the risk by avoiding hedges with large flat tops.

Renovating a hedge

Occasionally, particularly in a badly neglected or overgrown garden, you will need to give a hedge a new lease of life by cutting it back really hard. You will have to be quite ruthless to achieve this.

Timing, however, is extremely important. As a rule of thumb, most evergreens will stand cutting back hard into thick wood in the late spring. The exception is the yew, which will benefit from quite drastic treatment in mid to late summer.

Whatever the hedge, it will inevitably look bare for a season, but it is difficult to cause any long-term damage. The aesthetic drawback of rather bare branches will be more than compensated by the vibrant growth of regenerated plant material.

Where hedges have become overgrown or neglected, not every plant species can be renovated by such drastic treatment. However, if your hedge belongs to one of the groups given in the table to the right, then you can cut it back very hard with impunity.

This yew hedge not only provides excellent shelter from the elements — it is the ideal shape for coping with heavy falls of snow.

Hedge species that can be cut back really hard

Berberis thunbergii
Box (*Buxus*)
Escallonia
Hornbeam (*Carpinus*)
Hawthorn (*Crataegus*)
Privet (*Ligustrum*)
Beech (*Fagus*)

Pruning hedges

Plant a species or variety of tree that is suitable for hedging, and you will find no problem achieving a nice well-tailored effect.

If you trim the hedge so that the top is narrower than the bottom (as in the picture below), this will avoid damage occurring from heavy snowfall.

Root pruning

Occasionally fruit trees, particularly apples and pears, produce excessive growth to the detriment of crop production. This can sometimes be discouraged by restricting the root system by means of root pruning.

The procedure is as follows:

1 Mark out a circular trench about 2–4 ft (60–120 cm) from the base of the tree and about 18 in (40 cm) in width.

2 Dig to a depth of about 2 ft (60 cm) to reveal the root system.

3 Retain as much fibrous root as possible, but sever all large roots with a saw or mattock, and dispose of this thick material.

This operation is usually done in the winter. Occasionally the tree may need restaking.

Root pruning is well under way here — a large root is being severed, while the neighbouring fibrous roots are retained.

Root pruning

This method is sometimes used to prevent a tree or bush from producing over-exuberant growth.

The procedure is to dig a circular trench with a radius of approximately 5–10 ft (1.5–3 m) around the base of the tree. It should be about 18 in (45 cm) wide and 30 in (75 cm) deep. The root structures revealed are then chopped or sawn away, and the trench is refilled.

Dealing with bad pruning

Bad pruning is usually evident when you take over an old and neglected garden.

When large limbs have been damaged, possibly through high winds, it is advisable to employ the skills and expertise of a qualified tree surgeon.

In the case of more accessible small trees, bad pruning is usually evidenced by the preponderance of old wood and badly mutilated limbs. A pruning saw is usually the answer. With trees you should remove the offending fabric as close to the main trunk as possible, while shrubs must be cut down to ground level and old stumps should be eliminated. Most shrubs will stand this treatment.

Some very ugly growth can be obvious on some species of garden plants — it is better to remove this completely.

Below *A badly pruned specimen of ornamental cherry*

Above *The ugly mass of old wood on this rosemary plant is a sure sign of years of neglect.*

76

A pruning calendar

In order to grow plants successfully you must to large extent be governed by growing patterns and the seasons. Nevertheless, there is a temptation to be too pedantic and allow yourself to be persuaded that there is almost a 'holy writ' on the do's and don'ts of plant care.

In some instances, for example, it is easier to compile a list of don'ts rather than do's:

• Never cut back members of the plum family during the winter.

• Never cut live wood in a frozen state.

• With many deciduous trees you should avoid cutting into wood after mid-winter to minimise the risk of them bleeding.

Winter pruning

• Avoid storm damage to plants, particularly climbers, by tying in any loose branches.

• In early winter carry out any formative pruning.

• Coppicing and pollarding should be done in late winter.

• Rose shrubs can now be trimmed and dead-headed.

• It's also the time to prune autumn-fruiting raspberries.

Pruning is a year-round activity. This cherry laurel (Prunus laurocerasus) should be cut back hard in spring.

Spring pruning

• Clear out any storm-damaged wood and fallen branches.

• Coppicing and pollarding must be completed by early spring.

• If necessary prune deciduous trees that flower in late summer.

• Start trimming topiary.

• Prune shrubs back that flower on new wood.

• In mid-spring, prune shrubs that flower in winter or early spring.

• Prune deciduous climbers that flower on new wood.

• In late spring, prune any climbers that flower on old wood.

• Prune all bush, patio and miniatures roses, and trim back recurrent-flowering shrubs and climbers.

Summer pruning

• Ornamental trees that are spring-flowering should be pruned back now if this is prescribed.

• Pleached trees should be tied in and cut back.

• Clip topiary if necessary, and trim deciduous hedges in mid to late summer.

• Prune shrubs that flower on old wood, and also decorative hedges.

• Prune climbers that flower on old wood.

• In the rose garden, remove old flowering wood on Damasks and Gallicas.

• On fan-trained fruit trees, train shoots and remove very strong water shoots.

• 'Brutting' of cobnuts and filberts should be carried out in late summer.

• Prune summer-fruiting raspberries to encourage new canes.

• Summer-prune trained apples and pears.

Autumn pruning

• Any formative pruning of ornamental trees must be done now.

• The last trimming of hedges should be completed before the early frosts.

• In the rose garden, cut out old flowering wood on climbers and ramblers, and secure new wood.

• After the first frosts, cut bush roses down by a third to reduce storm damage.

• Remove old canes of blackberries and hybrid berries.

• Prune fan-trained peaches and nectarines after fruiting.

• Start winter-pruning apples, pears and bush fruits.

Where to see pruning demonstrated

Practical demonstrations of seasonal pruning are held at a variety of venues around the country to help the enquiring gardener.

The list that follows is not comprehensive, but with luck you should be able to find information about a demonstration at a venue not too far away from you.

The Royal Horticultural Society (RHS)

Wisley Gardens, Surrey

March: Rose pruning.

June: Shrub pruning.

July: Summer pruning of fruit trees and bushes.

November: Pruning of fruit trees and bushes.

Rosemoor, Torrington, North Devon

March: Planting, pruning and maintenance.

July: Summer pruning in the fruit and vegetable garden.

July: Summer pruning in the garden.

Hyde Hall, Retendon, Essex

July: Summer pruning of trees and shrubs.

October: Autumn pruning of rose ramblers, shrubs and climbers.

Pershore College of Horticulture, Worcestershire

February: Winter pruning of fruit trees.

March: Pruning ornamentals.

Note
Entrance to RHS events is by ticket only to both members and non-members, and must be booked in advance.

The Royal Horticultural Society's gardens at Wisley in Surrey are one of several places in the UK where pruning demonstrations are held. Wisley Gardens are worth a visit for the sake of the gardens alone.

The Royal National Rose Society (RNRS)

Gardens of the Rose, St Albans, Herts.

March: Rose pruning

October: Pruning and training of ramblers and climbers

These events are free to RNRS members; adult non-members are asked to pay a small fee.

Other societies
For readers in other parts of the UK, similar demonstrations are given by the **Northern Horticultural Society** at Harlow Carr near Harrogate in Yorkshire, and at the **Scottish Agricultural College** in Ayr, Scotland.

The Gardens of the Rose at St Albans in Hertfordshire are the home of the Royal National Rose Society. Pruning demonstrations are held here regularly both in spring and autumn.

In addition to this, there are garden societies in various parts of the country, many of which hold comprehensive lecture programmes during the winter months. They will always welcome new members.

Index